THE
ART OF
DYLAN

The Art of Dylan

F. E. Fram

F E FRAM

"Rush no more"

A time will come, know this for sure
No man will march that skyline, as before
And the winds will rush no more
And the winds will rush no more ...

Felsic faces won't hush the native cry
All as one, we'll some day die
Plutonic plagues from the staff above
Doane's dream, Lakotan love
Lincoln's lair behind the hair
Crazy Horse and his wild mare
Said father Borglum to his son
"Carry on the work I've begun"
Sixty feet from here to there
A hundred men, one stony stare

A time will come, know this for sure
No man will march that skyline, as before
And the winds will rush no more
And the winds will rush no more ...

F.E.Fram
May 2018

Forward by the author

A couple of years ago, I was invited to create a body of ekphrastic work as part of my Creative Writing studies. I decided to interrogate the imagination, lyrics and even cover-art of Bob Dylan in terms of ekphrasis and locate his achievement in that tradition.

In *The Gazer's Spirit*,[1] Hollander writes of the ways in which artworks are confronted by modern authors,[2] from "addressing the image, making it speak, speaking of it interpretively [and] meditating upon the moment of viewing it" (Hollander 1995). He contrasts this with the heavily descriptive output commonly seen from early Greek and Roman practitioners of this literary form.

For the creative challenge, the desire for unexpected results or perhaps to tie in with the subversive nature of the man at the centre of my writing, I aligned myself with the more modern branch of ekphrasis, as Hollander would view it. There is always a balance to be struck, however. I wanted to write beyond the fringes of formulaic orthodoxy, while simultaneously respecting this ancient poetic form's central traditions.

In this sense, albeit with more modest aspirations, I draw inspiration from Whistler's *Arrangement in Grey and Black No.1*[3]; a portrait painted with the subject in a side-on pose, rather than the more conventional front-facing position. Interestingly, her clothing and dour demeanour produce an image typical of a Victorian lady of her age and status. Nevertheless, it was controversial at the time. Yet since then, it has spawned many admirers from across the arts – sculptors such as Loester, novelists such as Don Delillo and composers such as Debussy all taking inspiration from it in their own creations.

Additionally, I decided my poems should have a common thread – replicating that encountered in *Lines of Vision* and *I Spy Pinhole Eye*, books I have drawn much inspiration from. The former uses a broad remit (art from Ireland's National Gallery), while the latter uses fixed-distance pylon photos shot through a pinhole camera. I knew I wanted something with the qualities of both to unite the seven pieces; i.e. the breadth that one would expect of an established art gallery and the niche of a slightly obscure subject matter.

Having initially experimented with writing on famous icons of "Americana", (with a piece on Mount Rushmore, *Rush no more,* which is shown on the book's dedication page) the next stage was to identify a sub-genre within contemporary American culture that might not be an obvious choice for ekphrastic writing – the art of Dylan.

Regardless of one's view on whether Dylan's lyrics contain sufficient literary merit to be deserving of serious academic discourse, there can be little doubt that Dylan's artistry[4] lends itself well to ekphrasis, connecting as it does the verbal and visual in often surreal and imaginative ways across the time-space continuum. Both in his own output and as the subject of other artists too, the artwork by and of Dylan seamlessly combines the idea of "the poet and the painter"[5] as almost one – a notion at the heart of ekphrasis itself.

The creative process is somewhat shrouded in mystery – some even attributing it to the invocation of muses and other forms of divination. There is little doubt that Dylan views it in this way when he sings to the *Mother of Muses* in his latest record, *Rough and Rowdy Ways* (2020); however, he is clearly no stranger to the ekphrastic tradition either. Growing up in Hibbing, Minnesota with an uncle who owned a number of movie theatres, Dylan is well-known for imbuing his lyrics with scenes of a cinematic nature.

Whatever the source, poets rarely produce work in isolation. Even a writer of T.S. Eliot's calibre (like Dylan a fellow Nobel laureate) recognised the role Ezra Pound had in the making of his 1925 edition of *The Waste Land,* calling his mentor *Il miglior fabbro.*[6] Of course, these two poets famously appear together in Dylan's *Desolation Row* forty years on – no longer in collaboration but "fighting in the captain's tower." In the spirit of recognising those from whom we draw guidance and inspiration, I wish to pay a particular tribute to Dr. Kelly Grovier, whose unstinting support and expert insight made this project a reality.

The poems presented here have thematic and stylistic commonalities and differences. They cover disparate artistic modalities, namely photography,[7] sculpture and painting.[8] As noted already, some are by Dylan himself,[9] others are not. Moreover, they take their inspiration from artwork at different points in Dylan's career. These choices were made so that my poems would not be monolithic, thereby reflecting the diversity of Dylan's cultural impact and the unbounded possibilities of ekphrastic writing.

In keeping with Dylan's own artistic output, holistically the pieces deal with themes of freedom, inner discovery, solitude, love, loss and aspiration, among others. These transcendent elements are amplified through the use of literary devices such as extended metaphors and pictorial tropes – for example, the symbolism of the road in *Endless highway* and the gates in *Unmasked and unnoticed*.

Stylistically, the work is replete with instances of double-negatives,[10] sentences starting with conjunctions and colloquialisms that are not often associated with poetry.[11] This is in keeping with Dylan's own approach to writing, which refuses to be constrained by literary convention, and it is consistent with his image as a counter-cultural icon who chooses to reflect the vernacular of the common American.

I lend authenticity to the poetic voice by mirroring this approach. For this reason, we see multiple contractions[12] and the breaking of grammatical rules with *'n all.* Dylan's diction is a strong influence here, with words and phrases from his lyrics being used throughout. For example, "fare thee well" famously features in Dylan's 1963 hit *Don't Think Twice, It's Alright* and is repeated in my poem *This land is your land*. Similarly, the word *'neath* is used extensively by Dylan[13] and is incorporated in both my *Forever young* and *Smile for me* offerings.

I acknowledge contemporary culture's influence through the use of words like "hip". This stands in contrast to archaic language like "whence" in *Highway 61 revisited*. This juxtaposition adds a sense of timelessness, through the direct merging of the current and past. In this sense, the ekphrastic writing is following on from Dylan acting as a bridge between old and new. We have Dylan's self-image as the indefatigable troubadour from the High Middle Ages on an endless tour, but also the man at the forefront of changing times, spearheading his generation into a bright dawn to come.

In addition to the anachronisms we see in Dylan's own work[14] making their way into the poems, the lexicon has also been necessarily influenced by the artwork's medium. We see reference to "acrylic dreams" in the mural-inspired *Forever young* and to "shutter" in the photo-based *Highway 61 revisited*, for instance.

Some poems are deliberately vague in parts.[15] This is so that the pieces are redolent of many of Dylan's most celebrated works, which are more surrealist in nature. In contrast, this ambiguity is not carried over into the more straightforward *This land is your land*, where the meaning does not require interpretation.

Occasionally, ekphrastic writing is only tangentially related to the artwork. In McGuiness' *A White Horse* after Gericault, the only detail linking the words to the image is the horse's colour. There is no mention of the materiality, for instance. It is almost a form of reverse notional ekphrasis – "I dreamt a white horse". I recapture the essence of this approach in the earlier drafts of *Smile for me* and *Endless highway* – creating near dream-like scenes, in which meditative narratives permeate. This allowed me as the narrator to mirror the artworks; going on a journey of self-discovery through the writing process and ultimately led me to expand the finished pieces reprinted here – to better establish connections with the source materials.

Given the subject matter, I made the conscious decision to include rhyme, musicality and overt lyricism in much of the writing.[16] However, I also set out to explore a range of styles. For example, the pace and rhythm in *Highway 61 revisited* is driven by occasionally using enjambment, rather than being derived from a reliance on a consistent rhyming scheme. I was keen to experiment with a lack of syntactical breaks as an alternative to end-stopped lines[17]– as, left unfettered, the latter has the potential to feel forced.

Although the poems have as their inspiration different media, each represents an attempt to make the artwork and the ekphrastic response contiguous. Put another way, each has at its foundation the "urge to merge". Similarly, I made the poems palpable through the use of puns, often relating to the materiality of the artwork. For example, "steely eyes" in reference to the metal gate in *Unmasked and unnoticed* and "idle" – a play on the concept of sculptures as objects of worship and even idolatry, with Guthrie acting as the figure that Dylan holds up as an idol of sorts in *This land is your land.*

Moreover, having made the physical realities of the artwork tangible, I often go beyond what can be seen. This "one-upmanship" is characteristic of much ekphrastic writing. A relevant influence would be Dylan contemporary and fellow Beat generation poet Ginsberg's *Cézanne's Ports.* I employ similar approaches, while being mindful not to lose the physicality of the art. Interestingly, *Cézanne's Ports* also impacted my decision to include the personification of "Eternity" in two poems.[18]

Continuing with influences, *Smile for me* is based on Dylan's *Portrait of a Woman Smiling*, which itself seems to pick up on his 1966 hit *Visions of Johanna.*[19] Clearly, this is a topic of some interest to Dylan, as it has been to countless others before. Undeniably, Pater's writing on the *Mona Lisa* and Dylan's own musings inform my ekphrastic writing here.

Although Eduardo Kobra's mural has attracted considerable critical review, it has not been the subject of ekphrastic poetry. The same can be said of Dylan's *Endless highway* painting and his iron gate sculpture. However, regarding the latter, clearly many have written about artwork featuring gates generally and specifically, the *Gates of Eden* – including Dylan himself. Familiarity with this work has likely affected my own writing, if only subliminally.

Turning to *This land is your land*, the lilting lyrical style echoes that found in Stevens' *The Man with the Blue Guitar (1937)* – a response to Picasso's 1903 painting, *The Old Guitarist* (Cheeke 2008). While there are obvious differences, I had both this image and Stevens' poem in mind while writing, as they deal with ageing musicians and their inevitable decline.

A fuller exposition of the inter-textuality must include reference to both Fuller's *The dice cup*, where we read: "in the winter garden, the snow on shoulders is heavier than their bronze" and reference to "Nor gates of steel so strong but Time decays?" from Shakespeare.[20] After all, no work on the "Shakespeare of Song" would be complete without mention of the Bard himself.

Although obviously not writing on Pam Taylor's sculpture in Warwickshire nor Dylan's ironwork in Maryland, Fuller and Shakespeare remind us how even the supposedly immortalised legacy of legends and the sturdiest of known substances, must give way to greater forces. The seasonality of celebrity and the susceptibility of every man-made structure to the ravages of time, are themes I elaborate on in my own work.

Finally, there is often a tension between the pure abstraction of an artist like Pollock and the hyper-naturalism we see in a painting like *Betty*, by Richter. The same holds true in the written response to such artworks. In choosing Dylan as my poetry's subject, I knew this tension would be slightly different, but no less intractable. Namely, how does one remove the music (Dylan's "naturalist" state) from the art (the "abstract" embodiment of the music)? I have not battled with this; instead, I embraced it as an opportunity to include numerous nods to Dylan's inspiring writing throughout the ekphrastic pieces. I hope you enjoy reading the work as much as I have enjoyed writing it.

F. E. Fram
July 2020

References

Hollander, J., 1995. *The Gazer's Spirit: Poems Speaking to Silent Works of Art* (p. 7). Chicago: University of Chicago Press.
Cheeke, S., 2008. *Writing for Art: The Aesthetics of Ekphrasis*. Manches

[1] a collection of ekphrastic poems
[2] In this quotation, Hollander is referring nineteenth and twentieth century writers as "modern"
[3] commonly referred to as *Whistler's Mother*
[4] both that directly created by him and that relating to him but made by others

[5] a lyrical excerpt from Dylan's song *Chimes of Freedom* (1964)

[6] the better craftsman – a phrase borrowed from Dante

[7] one black and white, one colour image

[8] one canvas, one mural

[9] two of the three paintings

[10] "when you don't see me no more" and "I ain't lookin' back no more" in *Smile for me*, for example

[11] such as "ain't", "gonna" and "outta"

[12] such as gatherin' and gettin'

[13] such as in his song *Gates of Eden*: All except when 'neath the trees of Eden

[14] such as in "Come all ye fair and tender ladies"

[15] particularly those inspired by Dylan's own creations, such as *Unmasked and unnoticed*

[16] we see choral repetition in *Smile for me*, for example

[17] in which words are chosen to form neat couplets

[18] *Unmasked and unnoticed* and *Endless highway*

[19] the song features the line: Mona Lisa must have had the highway blues – you can tell by the way she smiles

[20] excerpt from *Since brass, nor stone, nor earth, nor boundless sea*

Highway 61 revisited

"Mr. Dylan will see you now."
We'll see him evermore.
Wally's there too somehow,
but Bob's always in the fore.
With contemptuous quiver at the lip;
an aborted quiff, says "I'm not so hip."
Then suddenly the silence sliced,
whence once riddle and rhyme came
together.
And, to a pin-prick point
They sent their eyes.
For the freedom, they followed his;
unsheltered for the especial moment.
And, puncturing the void
with a singular shutter sound,
the artist capturing the artist
completely.
The face - its lines locked in time;
in step with the voice of a generation,
wearing a t-shirt reading:
"We all like motorcycles
To some degree ..."
Yet I abandoned mine,
many revolutions ago.

Highway 61 revisited, album cover photo (1965)
Photographer: Daniel Kramer Location: Gramercy Park, New York

Forever young

My image
harassed at the Hennepin
Corner with Fifth.
The crowds gatherin'
needing a lift
at Eduardo's concept;
from canvass to wall
his five so adept
at brushes, rollers 'n all.
Scaffolding and ladders
reaching five stories tall.
Paint: water-borne,
a hard rain's gonna fall.

I'm down from stage to street.
Acrylic dreams, not so discreet.
Emblazoned lyrics, now obsolete.
I pose: pre-crash, post-crash.
I rose: a phoenix from the ash.
In psychedelic scandals, I splash;
'neath fedora hat, my hidden stash
of unknown truths.

They're here,
not understanding what they see.
I'm here,
thinking is this really me?
A pawn in their game
upon mired mosaic board.
A fortnight to reclaim
and claim
"For the people", restored.

Aspect ratio: not golden;
glistens nonetheless.
Listens, not beholden
for grid paper blocks know best
what each forgotten face
would say unto the other.
Am I returning to a place
I've never been, mother;
or some place I've never left?

An aged soul's quashed quietude
Overpainted: layered with lassitude,
like a former President nude in solitude
with a world he left wholly
unwholesome.
I was older then - younger now;
as they climb each rung.
They climb to keep me keepin' on.
They climb to keep me forever young ...

Eduardo Kobra - Dylan, 2015.
Photography by Bill Hickey.

Judas on tour

Aust's away, she's sailing from afar!
Barry wants a snap photo,
though the electric violin's in the car.
The bike's on desolation row,
where Casanova's mouth is still ajar.
"Keep to the left this time!"
sinister Judas is on tour.
"Take it right, Feinstein!"
"Ok, I'll do one more".
The merry men and Einstein,
they'll be in the next one for sure.
Like one of the seven wonders,
all blurry in the cloud;
no, the heart don't grow fonder,
the beats just get so loud!
So says Alan in blonde on blonder,
reaping what's not been ploughed.
But the rainy road to my 12:35 ends right here
and the direction home still ain't clear ...

Cover photo for No direction home (2005)

Unmasked and unnoticed

I make it sixteen by twenty-five,
there's plenty here to keep me alive.
The fabric of choice - sheet metal unsold.
I better get to Cannery Row, before I'm too old.
"See Eden's gates in Bob's ferric fold!"
That's what the papers will state
or something about a tangled, twist of fate.

Scrap coins to feed the bandit boys,
they make 'em outta guns and toys.
Scrap words from the junkyard jukebox
say there's no time for second-hand clocks.
But these cogs won't stop for no one!
All my life, welding words to stand the fire to come.
Now I'll leave it all by the western gate,
for the many to walk right on by.
But you'll know them from their sullen state
and as the "how" to your "why" ...

"Here he comes from the iron range!"
Some say prophet, others how strange!
Don't trust him, with those steely eyes.
All the better to plunder and plagiarise?
Sad-eyed Sara, forever at my gate;
I made it for you, so must I wait?
Some will think it an act of love,
I just couldn't remove spanner from glove!

Am I locked in or are you locked out?
Sara, tell me what this is all about.
In time with industry's marching band;
I'm chained too, but I'll lend a hand.
Through and through, spikes and holes.

With the wheels of time – on we roll,
on we roll, on we roll.
As through the gates,
Eternity strolls,
unmasked and unnoticed.

**"Portal" at Maryland's MGM's National Harbor Casino by
Bob Dylan**
Photography by Sean Kelley.

This land is your land

I dreamed of a meadow
some mythical land
Always in your shadow
a guitar in my hand

I walked in the wood
and what did I see?
I walked where she stood
sculpting Guthrie and me

I'll write you a song
a fare-thee-well
It won't take long
I'm under your spell

She made you of bronze
idle lying where the lady lay
We speak of bygones
what it'd take to make you stay

Dream with me, o! Guthrie
Tell me of these lands
Bound for glory, our destiny
With guitars in our hands ...

Sculptor in Stratford-upon-Avon, England

Smile for me

Crude coal is breathing actuality
Papa's penance from 'neath the floor
Scarlet lips painted so feathery
Concealing eyes only I can adore
Smile so sweet like you did before
When you don't see me no more
Just smile sweet like you did before ...

Write these words down for me
I don't own them anymore
It's gettin' too close to just let it be
Ain't clear what I'm searchin' for ...
Smile so sweet like you did before
When you don't see me no more
Just smile sweet like you did before ...

Take what's gone by from me
I ain't lookin' back no more
It's gettin' too dark to see
The ghosts are gatherin' at my door ...
Smile so sweet like you did before
When you don't see me no more
Just smile sweet like you did before ...

Lift this weight from off of me
I can't carry it no more
It's gettin' too heavy, set me free
I'm prayin' with my knees to the floor ...
Smile so sweet like you did before
When you don't see me no more
Just smile sweet like you did before ...

Smile your smile again for me
We can't laugh like we did before
The day is closin' with your beauty
How could I ever ask for any more?
Smile so sweet like you did before
When you don't see me no more
Just smile sweet like you did before ...

Portrait of a Woman Smiling
Artist: Bob Dylan

Endless highway

I turned aside the great divide,
first this way and now that.
I never left but they say I've arrived,
demanding directions at the drop of a hat.
I turned to see the changing sky;
all crimson, honey and rust.
Down the same road, who knows why;
better figure it out before we turn to dust.

I turned my eyes to the top of the hill,
where a lonely flag did stand.
I turned my ears to the wind but it blew so still,
as I stood where the sea meets the sand.
I turned my dreams towards His will,
then headed for the land.

I turned my hand to toil the land,
but only dust and stone it returned.
I turned on my heel for one last stand,
to bone and skin with nothing learned.
I turned my fears to His command,
now there's no need to be concerned.

I turned to reach all the truths,
as pearls for the pigs below.
I turned towards the steps of my youth,
Eternity has time to kill, that I much know.
I turned to silence the streams of my heart,
let us forever grow but never apart.

I turned to wait at the sea of snow,
aside trains with no place to go.
I turned to the peaks of the Pyrenees,

their beauty will have you on your knees!
I turned to say goodbye to the graces of the Lord,
and all the joys we could never afford.

I turned and turned to stumble on stones,
desolation deep to the marrow of bones.
I turned away though He did call,
ignoring starry nights that make you feel small.
I turned to silence the streams of my heart,
let us forever love like it was the start.

We turn to the road as it takes you and I
to the same destination, though a different place.
Now there's nothing we will ever pass by
which cannot be replaced.
The road turns my mind back to Pa,
did he travel it in vain?
The road carries on without you Ma;
this painting's all that remains …

Endless highway (2017)
Artist: Bob Dylan

Copyright information

1. Highway 61 revisited, album cover photo (1965); Photographer: Daniel Kramer; Location: Gramercy Park, New York. The cover art copyright is believed to belong to the label, Columbia, or the graphic artist(s).
2. Eduardo Kobra - Dylan, 2015. Photography by Bill Hickey.
3. Cover photo for No direction home (2005). The cover art copyright is believed to belong to the distributor, Paramount Pictures, the publisher of the video or the studio which produced the video. The picture shows Dylan at the Aust Ferry on the Bristol Channel in May 1966. The ferry closed that year, to be replaced by the Severn Bridge (just visible in the mist, to the right behind the car). When the complete picture was reproduced in 'The Guardian' of 22nd July 2005, the credit line was to Barry Feinstein (photographer).
4. "Portal" at Maryland's MGM's National Harbor Casino by Bob Dylan. Photography by Sean Kelley.
5. Garden of Heroes and Villains in Stratford-upon-Avon, England; Sculptor: Pam Taylor. Photography ©jacquemart.
6. Portrait of a Woman Smiling; Artist: Bob Dylan. Courtesy of Black Buffalo Collection.
7. Endless highway (2017); Artist: Bob Dylan.

Bookcover Eduardo Kobra - Dylan, 2015. Photography by Bill Hickey.